Chinese Wushu Series

MW01282115

# Basics of Spear Play

*Qiu Pixiang*

FOREIGN LANGUAGES PRESS    BEIJING

First Edition 1999
Translated by Zhang Tingquan

Home Page:
http://www.flp.com.cn
E-mail Addresses:
info@flp.com.cn
sales@flp.com.cn

ISBN 7-119-01392-0

© Foreign Languages Press, Beijing, China, 1999

Published by Foreign Languages Press
24 Baiwanzhuang Road, Beijing 100037, China

Printed by Beijing Foreign Languages Printing House
19 Chegongzhuang Xilu, Beijing 100044, China

Distributed by China International Book Trading Corporation
35 Chegongzhuang Xilu, Beijing 100044, China
P.O. Box 399, Beijing, China

*Printed in the People's Republic of China*

# Content

# Chapter One    General Description

Spear play is one of the major martial arts using long-shaft Chinese Wushu weapons. It originated as an ancient Chinese weapon used for attacking at a distance.

It is recorded that there were "lance, spear, halberd, the Qiu spear and the Yi spear" as early as the times when society was still organized in clans. These five weapons are generally termed the five arms. The Qiu spear is a short-shaft spear, and the Yi spear has a four-meter-long-shaft. If the shaft was too long, the spear was unwieldy, but even ordinary ancient spears are longer than those of today. Wars were frequent in the Spring and Autumn Period and the Warring States Period, more than 2,000 years ago. When two armies met in their battle chariots, they often used spears for attack. The heads of the ancient spears that have been unearthed are generally much broader than the heads of modern spears, and some have double-winged blades. By the time of the Qin and Han dynasties, around 2,000 years ago, the spearhead became smaller and narrower, approximately the size of modern spearheads.

During the Jin Dynasty in the third and fourth centuries, bronze spears were developed in China. They were later replaced by iron spears. In time, long-shaft spears and swords replaced iron halberds and lances as major battlefield weapons. During the Song Dynasty about 1,000 years ago, the lance and halberd were altogether abandoned and the spear became the exclusive long-shaft weapon.

The spear techniques used in battle were called "the art of the battle spear." Some masters gradually developed a set of spear-play techniques incorporating artistic values for competi-

1

tion. This became known as "sport spear" for its varied techniques which required a solid mastery of basic skills. In time, 17 different schools of spear play were developed such as the Yang Family Spear, the Sha Family Spear, the Ma Family Spear, the Cheng Family Spear and the E'mei Spear. All these schools of spear play are recorded in books on Chinese Wushu. A special book entitled *On Arms Techniques* was written by Wu Shu in the early Qing Dynasty (1644-1911), combining the theory and technique of spear play.

However, the spear play practiced today in Chinese Wushu is neither the "battle spear" nor the "sport spear" of the past. With the introduction of modern firearms, the battle spear was used less and less for military purposes while it gained popularity as a medium for physical exercise. By summing up their spear play experience, masters developed them into routines or sets of exercises for physical fitness. These exercises have been termed "spear play routines" and are recognized as the embodiment of modern spear play. As these routines are performed more and more often at exhibitions, spear masters have been encouraged to refine their techniques, creating what has come to be called the "flowery spear." In these exercises there are more consecutive changes in technique and more varied stances and footwork. There are also many movements and jumps with purely aesthetic value. From practical point of view, modern spear play has less value, but from the point of view of sports and aesthetics, it has increased in value. Spear play with its physical exertion and varied techniques is an art in itself, an art demonstrating the ability of the human body, and the qualities as well as the skills of human beings.

With Wushu becoming more popular, spear play has become one of the major long-shaft weapon events in competitive programs. It is totally different from what it was in the ancient times, but there is still a connection between them. Spear play originated in ancient warfare, and its basic techniques have re-

2

mained essentially the same despite all apparent changes. The parries, thrusts, and pointing techniques remain the basic techniques of modern spear play. Mere figure play and jumps, without demonstrating basic techniques, are nothing more than an acrobatic performance. When practised as a sport, it must show the traditional features of combat movements.

There are also differences in the structures of spear weapons between those of today and those used in the past. Not only were the old spearheads large and varied, the shafts were also longer. The shaft of the modern spear, in most cases, is about the length of the human body plus the length of the extended arm. Larger spears exist, but they are not seen in competitions, only on rare demonstration occasions.

The main structural elements of the spear are the shaft, the head, and the tassel. The spearhead is now made of steel, but was made of bronze in ancient times. It is diamond-shaped, the front edges are sharp blades and it has a sharp point. The rear end is thicker and stronger, with a ridge in the middle. At the end of the head is a tube that can be put on the shaft, and in the middle of the tube is a small hole for a screw to affix it to the shaft. (Fig. 1-1)

The shaft is generally made of hardwood, mostly white wax wood which is hard, straight, and resilient.

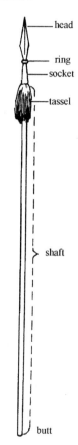

Fig. 1-1

3

The wood chosen must be straight and have small nodes. The front part should be thin and the rear thick, to provide a suitable grip.

The shaft is divided into three parts: The end part, the thickest, is called the spear root; the middle part is called the spear waist, and the upper part closest to the head is called the spear chest. In modern spear play, the common terms are spear butt and spear body (also called the middle and front parts).

In modern competition, the length of the spear is required to be body height plus the length of the fully extended arm. The spear body should not be too thin or too soft. If it is, it will be difficult to demonstrate proper spear-play techniques. In competition, there are special requirements for the spear body: the diameter of the spear body below the middle line must not be smaller than 2.29 cm for men and 2.13 cm for women; and it must not be smaller than 2.13 cm for boys and 2.03 cm for girls.

In preparing a shaft, it is best to retain the original wood. After it is chosen, it is enough just to cut off the nodes. The spear body should then be polished with sandpaper. It is most desirable to keep the fibrous bark. If the shaft is too thick, just cut off a thin cover. If too much is cut off, and only the heartwood is left, it may become fragile and is apt to bend or even break. The shaft should be smooth so the player can slide his hands to change grips and techniques.

The butt should be thick so the player can hold it tightly and exert force when thrusting. Some players like to wrap adhesive tape around the butt to prevent slipping. This is not desirable, however, since it is a weapon and nothing else should be added to it.

The joint between the head tube and the shaft should be decorated with a tassel. Generally, the tassel is made from a horse's tail hair or oxtail hair dyed red. A story goes that the tassels of ancient weapons were used mainly for practical purposes. This was because after an enemy soldier was killed on the battlefield, the blood would run down with the tassel to avoid staining the shaft and the hands. It is also been said that the tassel was a decoration to demonstrate one's heroism and bravery. When the troops lined up before going into battle the tassels danced in the breeze to heighten their fighting spirit. In modern spear play, the tassel remains as a symbol. It can help to clearly demonstrate spear techniques, such as the inward and outward parry and the spear coil.

## Chapter Two    Basic Techniques

There is a Wushu saying that "The spear is used like a straight line, while cudgel play covers a large range," and "the spear looks like an undulating dragon while the cudgel is wielded like raindrops." It is clear that spear play stresses accuracy, smoothness and agility.

First of all, attention should be paid to the correct manner of holding the spear. As described in ancient books, when holding the spear, "the front hand should serve as a tube and the rear hand as a lock." In other words, the front hand should be loose and the rear hand should be tight. In spear play, it is taboo to release the butt from the rear hand. In other words, the rear hand should hold the whole root of the shaft, and it is incorrect to leave some part of the butt behind the little finger. For one reason, if this is done the shaft will not form a straight line with the arm; for another reason, the spear is supposed to thrust at the opponent, and if rear hand has no power to hold and push it, this will greatly reduce the thrusting power; and for the third reason, the weapon will then be shortened and the player will not be able to make full use of the length of the weapon. The correct method is to hold the end of the butt with the rear hand, slightly behind the butt, so that it is supported by the center of the palm. But it should not be held too far back or it will affect the power of the five fingers holding it. (Fig. 2-1)

The front hand should be placed around the middle of the spear body, with the four fingers in the snail shape. (Fig. 2-2) Whether the spear should be held tightly or loosely depends on the changes of movements during play. For example, when in a parry or flick, the spear should be held first loosely and then tightly, with the movement of the rear hand. In the downward cut, the spear should also be held tightly. However, in the coil and piercing movements the shaft should be held loosely.

Fig. 2-1

Fig. 2-2

  Apart from holding the spear, it is also important to slip the hands and change grips. Otherwise, it will be difficult to demonstrate "the spear moving like an undulating dragon" feature of spear play. In the shuttle-moving spear and cloud spear, the movements of hand slipping and changing grips must be quick and nimble, with the shaft not held too tightly. However, neither should it be held too loosely. If held too loosely, the spear might slip out of the hands during quick movements. This must always be avoided. Therefore, the hold must be firm and nimble and adaptable to changing conditions. An old saying goes: "One month's practice for the cudgel, one year's practice for the sword, and longer practice for the spear."

7

Therefore, the practice of spear play is most difficult and flexibility is essential when holding the spear. Only through constant practice and the acquisition of the basic skills is it possible to hold the spear both skillfully and with freedom.

After learning the techniques, it is important to use them in practice. The main techniques of spear play are the outward parry, the inward parry, the thrust, the downward cut, and pointing, flicking, lifting, piercing, the upward parry, and coiling and bumping. The main butt techniques include butt cutting, butt raising, and butt slamming.

### 1. outward and inward parries:

The outward and inward parries, together with the thrust, are the three main basic spear-play techniques.

The outward and inward parries are defensive techniques to ward off the attacks from long-shaft weapons. The outward parry is for warding off attack from left and the inward parry is for warding off attack from right.

The basic stance for the outward and inward parries includes standing with feet apart to a half squat to form the semi-horse riding step, left tiptoe obliquely forward, with the body weight in the center and slightly backward, on the right side of the right foot. Hold the spear with both hands, the rear hand against the right side of the waist, left arm slightly bent and at the middle of the spear body.

When parrying outward, hold the spear with the right hand and turn the wrist inward, palm downward and outward from inside. Move the left hand and turn the wrist inward and upward, palm up, combining the force of the hands to circle the spearhead counterclockwise, not higher than the head, nor lower than the hips, and power focused on the outer edge of the front part of the spear.

When parrying inward, shift the body weight slightly forward. Hold the spear with the right hand with the wrist turned

8

outward so the palm is turned back inward. Hold the spear with the left hand and turn it inward so the palm is turned downward. Combine the force of the two hands to circle the spearhead clockwise, not higher than the head nor lower than the hips, and power focused on the lower edge of the front part of the spear. (Fig. 2-3, 2-4, 2-5)

## 2. thrust

The thrust is the most important and most basic spear-play technique. It is used to thrust the spearhead at all parts of the opponent's body. A thrust at any part of the body at or above shoulder level is called the upper thrust, and a thrust at any part at or below knee level is called the lower thrust. A thrust with the shaft at or above chest level is called the upper horizontal thrust, a thrust with the shaft between the chest and the waist is called the middle horizontal thrust, and a thrust at or below waist level is called the lower horizontal thrust, A thrust only 20 centimeters above the ground is called the lower horizontal thrust.

"The middle horizontal thrust is the king of all thrust techniques in spear play." In this book, much space is devoted to describing the proper method of executing the middle horizontal thrust. All other thrust techniques will be easier to learn once this thrust technique is grasped.

In executing the middle horizontal thrust, hold the spear with both hands by the side of the waist and bend the legs to a half squat to form the semi-horse-riding stance. While shifting the body weight forward and turning the waist to the left, straighten the rear leg to form the left bow step. At the same time, hold the spear with the right hand and thrust it straight forward from the right side of the waist and past the front of the upper abdomen. Slip the left hand backward to before the right hand and keep them in touch. Straighten the rear leg to exert the force together with the turning of the waist, and focus the force on the spearhead so that the spear shakes naturally. The

Fig. 2-3

Fig. 2-4

Fig. 2-5

tiptoe, the spearhead and the tip of the nose should face the same direction. After the spear is thrusted, keep the shoulders level and drop them with the body. Do not shrug or slant the shoulders. (Fig. 2-6, 2-7)

Fig. 2-6

Fig. 2-7

Fig. 2-7(part)

In the routines, there is also a movement of single-handed thrust. Usually, after holding the spear with both hands, loosen the left-hand grip and thrust with the right hand. When thrusting with a single hand horizontally, hold the spear with the hands crossed before the chest and thrust it with the right hand after loosen the left-hand grip, the right arm forming a straight line with the shaft, power focused on the spearhead. (Fig. 2-8, 2-9)

Fig. 2-8

Fig. 2-9

12

### 3. point

It is one of the attacking techniques. It is used more often to attack the wrists, heads, shoulders and knees of the opponent with the spearhead.

In executing the point technique, slip the front hand slightly backward, and combine the force of both hands to attack with the spearhead from above downward. Exert the force for a short moment, and focus it on the spearhead. (Fig. 2-10, 2-11) There are upper, horizontal, and lower points, defined according to their different positions and directions. The upper point is not higher than head level, while the lower point is not higher than knee level or lower than ground level. The horizontal point is not higher than shoulder level or lower than hip level.

### 4. flick

The flick is used together with the points. It is a technique used to exert force for a brief moment and can be employed either for attack or defense.

In executing the flick technique, drop the point of the spearhead slightly and slip the left hand slightly forward, holding the spear tightly all of a sudden. Combine the force of both hands for a short moment to flick the spearhead upward, with the force focused on the spearhead and the shaft. (Fig. 2-11, 2-12) You can also flick horizontally to the left or right. In the upper flick, the spearhead is not higher than head level. In the horizontal flick, it is not higher than chest level or lower than waist level. In the lower flick, it is not higher than knee level or lower than ground level.

During practice, flicks can be practised together with points so you may understand the explosive force of the movements. ( Fig. 2-10, 2-11, 2-12)

### 5. downward cut

This is also an attacking technique with movement covering a large range . It is quick and powerful and includes fore-

Fig. 2-10

Fig. 2-11

Fig. 2-12

hand, backhand and swinging cuts.

In executing the cutting movements, hold the spear with both hands and raise it above the head. In practice, move the spear downward in the cutting form powerfully, while moving the front foot forward as the rear foot executes a follow-up step, power focused on the spearhead and the front part of the shaft. (Fig. 2-13, 2-14) In executing the forehand cut, keep the palm of the front hand forward and downward. In executing the backhand cut, keep the palm of the front hand inward and upward. (Fig. 2-17, 2-18) In executing the swinging cut, combine the downward cut with the swinging of the spear in a vertical circle.

### 6. upward thrust

This is used both for attack and defense, but mainly for attack. The upward thrust movement covers a large range.

In executing the upward thrust, hold the spear with both hands and thrust upward forcefully from below, power focused on the spearhead. (Fig. 2-14, 2-15, 2-16) There are forward upward thrusts and oblique upward thrusts. In the forward thrust, the spear is thrust upward in the forward direction, while in the oblique thrust the spear is thrust obliquely upward from one side. These can be practised together with the downward cut to get a feel for the force point of the spear.

### 7. parry

The parry is a technique used mainly for defense. There are upward parries, horizontal parries and downward parries defined according to their positions, and turning parries and cloud parries defined by the way they are executed.

In executing the parry, slip the front hand slightly and combine the force of both hands to move the spear to and fro lightly and smoothly, within a limited range of movement. When the parry is nearing completion, keep the front hand grip firm after slipping it, with power focused on the front part of

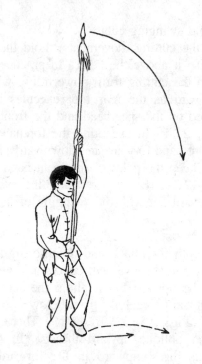

Fig. 2-13

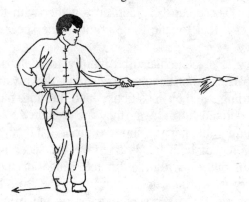

Fig. 2-14

Fig. 2-15

Fig. 2-16

17

Fig. 2-17

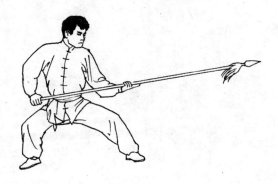

Fig. 2-18

the spear. In the upper parry, the spearhead is slightly above head level. In the horizontal parry, the point is not higher than chest level and not lower than waist level. In the lower parry, the point is not higher than knee level and not lower than ground level. In practicing the parry, combine it with the back cross step and the side step. (Fig. 2-19, 2-20, 2-21)

The turning parry is a horizontal or downward parry coordinated with the turning of the body.

The cloud parry is a parry immediately following the movement of the spear in a circle like a cloud floating over the head. In practice, this movement can be executed continuously. (Fig. 2-22, 2-23, 2-24, 2-25)

### 8. piercing

This is an attacking technique which is first used for defense and then for attack. Piercing can be applied from the throat, around the waist and behind the back.

When piercing, keep a loose grip with the front hand and deliver the spear with the rear hand. Be sure and take time to hold the spear butt securely when the spear is sent forward. Piercing must be quick, smooth, and executed without interruption, with the power focused on the spearhead. The spear must be close to the body as it is moved past it. When piercing from the throat, for example, the spear should be close by the throat, with the body bent backward slightly to dodge the attacking spear. At the same time, it should be executed quickly to attack the target. In piercing, the rear hand should exert the force properly. Especially in executing the behind-the-back piercing movement, the spear should be allowed to fly off both hands. If the spear flies too quickly or too far, it is difficult for the other hand to catch hold of the butt.

Usually, piercing from the throat and piercing from around the waist can be practised together. (Fig. 2-26, 2-27, 2-28, 2-29, 2-30) The behind-the-back piercing move should be practiced from a fixed position at the beginning, and then

Fig. 2-19

Fig. 2-20

Fig. 2-21

Fig. 2-22

Fig. 2-23

21

Fig. 2-24

Fig. 2-25

practiced using footwork. (Fig. 2-31, 2-32, 2-33, 2-34, 2-35, 2-36)

## 9. coiling

Coiling is a defensive technique. Coil the spear continuously to prevent an attack from the opponent. There are both inward and outward coiling. Inward coiling goes clockwise, and outward coiling goes counterclockwise.

In coiling, both hands should exert force gently and in a coordinated way to move the spearhead in vertical circles. When coiling, instead of moving both hands at the same time, you should mainly move the rear hand, with the front hand assisting the coiling so the spearhead has the power to coil. The coil should not be too large. If it is, it becomes loose. Generally, the coil should not be higher than shoulder level or lower than hip level. (Fig. 2-37, 2-38, 2-39)

## 10. vertical figure circling

This is a common movement in spear play routines, used during connections and transitions between movements. Executing the figures with a forward step, for example, connects the inward and outward parries, thrusting downward with a turn of the body and swinging cut and shoulder spear. To execute smooth and uninterrupted connections, you must have correct and perfect basic circling skills.

The basic movements: Grip the middle of the spear with both hands, with the radials opposite each other. Combine the force of the hands to move the spearhead and parry downward to outside the left leg while moving the butt of the spear to outside the right leg. In parrying downward, press the spear forward and downward to the left with the right hand, and to the right with the left hand so that the spear circles vertically on both sides of the body by the inertia of the downward parry. The left hand (front hand) grip should be flexible. In parrying downward, simply use the thumb and forefinger to grip the spear so that the movement is smooth and close to the body.

Fig. 2-26

Fig. 2-27

Fig. 2-28

Fig. 2-29

Fig. 2-30

Fig. 2-31

26

Fig. 2-32

Fig. 2-33

Fig. 2-34

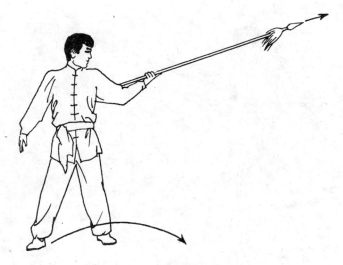

Fig. 2-35

28

Fig. 2-36

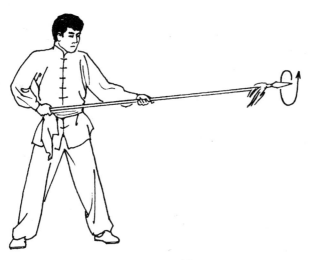

Fig. 2-37

29

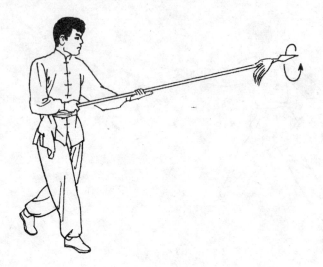

Fig. 2-38

Fig. 2-39

(Fig. 2-40, 2-41, 2-42, 2-43, 2-44, 2-45)

Start with the standing exercise. Stand with the feet apart, right foot in front. When parrying downward from left to right, shift the body weight forward and twist the body to the right, left heel slightly raised so that you can circle vertically close to your body to form figures on both sides.

After you become good at the standing exercise, you can learn to circle figures with walking steps. The circling movements should be well coordinated with the steps. Usually, you move the steps before executing the downward parry. For example, move the left step forward before executing the left downward parry, and move the right step forward before executing the right downward parry.

On this basis, you can do the figure circling with back cross step and body turnover, and circling with a rising uppercut, forward step, and body turn.

### 11. horizontal figure circling

This is a defensive spear technique, used mainly to guard against attacks from the opponent at above shoulder level. Horizontal circling is usually connected with the upward parry, upward outward parry, and push.

The basic movements: Grip the shaft of the spear at the middle and rear with both hands, arms crossed and the right hand under the left armpit, and use the left hand to move the spearhead from the front to the right and backward on a horizontal level so that the arms cross each other before the head, and circle the spear overhead one and a half circles, with the left hand under the right armpit and the spear butt in front of the body. (Fig. 2-46, 2-47, 2-48, 2-49, 2-50)

You can also circle figures from the opposite direction back to under the left armpit. After grasping the technique of circling the spear horizontally, you can wield the spear in different ways by using other techniques.

Fig. 2-40

Fig. 2-41

Fig. 2-42

Fig. 2-43

33

Fig. 2-44

Fig. 2-45

34

Fig. 2-46

Fig. 2-47

Fig. 2-48

Fig. 2-49

Fig. 2-50

## 12. shoulder spear

This is a variation technique in spear play routines, often used after the vertical figure circling. After using the shoulder spear, you can do attacking movements like the downward cut and pointing.

The basic movements: Grip the spear with both hands on the right side of the body and circle it 360 degrees, with the spearhead up by moving it forward, downward and backward, and with the right hand exerting force to move the spear across the back and the left shoulder. By using the inertia of the circling and using the right hand to lift it upward, the spear rolls across the left shoulder to in front of the body. First use the left hand to receive the shaft, then take the right hand off the shaft and grip the butt of the spear again with the right hand in front of the body. (Fig. 2-51, 2-52, 2-53, 2-54, 2-55)

You can also move the spear across the back and the right shoulder. Be sure to exert the force properly, and roll the shaft tightly across the shoulder. The change of grips should be well-timed. Beginners often drop the shaft, but after you practise it repeatedly you will be able to move it across freely at will.

Fig. 2-51

Fig. 2-52

Fig. 2-53

Fig. 2-54

39

### 13. sweep

This is an attacking technique for using the spearhead to sweep the knees, ankles, and feet of the opponent.

Its movements are somewhat similar to those of the downward parry, but the movements are much larger and the force is also exerted differently. It calls for initiative, quickness and power when attacking. The basic movements: Hold the spear with both hands, use the power generated by twisting the waist and from the arms to keep the front end of the spear close to the ground and sweep horizontally from right to left or from left to right. This movement is usually executed with low stances like crouching, squatting, and bow stance. (Fig. 2-56, 2-57)

Fig. 2-55

Fig. 2-56

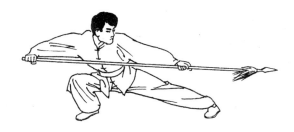

Fig. 2-57

### 14. bump

This is a close-range attacking technique. When the opponent's body is close to yours, point and cut techniques cannot be used, and bumping is then most desirable.

The basic movements: Use one hand to pull the spear backward, slip the other hand to the part connecting the shaft and spearhead, with the radial facing the spear butt, and bump the opponent like a dagger. There are upper, middle, and lower bumping moves. Upper bumping is executed at throat level, middle bumping between the chest and the waist, and lower bumping between the crotch and the knees. (Fig. 2-58, 2-59, 2-60)

Pulling with the rear hand and slipping the front hand to the spear chest prior to bumping are also called drawing. (Fig. 2-58, 2-59)

### 15. slam and low-stance press

These are attacking techniques, used mainly to attack the opponent from a long distance or to dodge an attack.

The basic movements for the slam: Hold the spear overhead with both hands, and slam forward and downward forcefully with one hand, or with both hands, so that the spear beats the ground horizontally. (Fig. 2-61, 2-62)

Fig. 2-58

Fig. 2-59

Fig. 2-60

The basic movements for the low-stance press: Hold the spear with both hands, press it downward from above horizontally and lower the body weight so that the spear lies horizontally, close to the ground. (Fig. 2-63, 2-64)

In both the slam and low-stance press, keep the spear level while dropping it. Slamming should be quick and powerful.

Fig. 2-61

Fig. 2-62

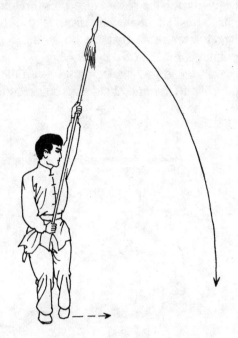

Fig. 2-63

Fig. 2-64

### 16. butt techniques

In spear play, the spearhead is generally used for attack in most cases, but sometimes the butt is also used for attack. Especially in repeated attacks, both the head and the butt are used to gain time and overwhelm the opponent. When you are close to the opponent, you can use the butt for both attack and defence.

The common butt techniques include jabbing with the butt, striking horizontally with the butt, raising the butt, and slamming the butt.

Jabbing is used mainly to attack the head, chest, and abdomen of the opponent. The basic movements: Slip the right hand back to the rear of the spear, and use the shaft to hit straight and horizontally to the right or to the left, powerfully with both hands, and with the power focused on the end of the spear butt. (Fig. 2-65, 2-66)

Horizontal butt striking is used mainly to hit the head, ribs, and waist of the opponent. The basic movements: Draw the spear backward with the right hand and slip it to the middle and rear of the shaft with a forward step to strike horizontally with the butt from right to left, or from left to right, with the power focused on the rear of the spear. (Fig. 2-67, 2-68, 2-69)

Fig. 2-65

45

The raising of the butt is used mainly to hit the lower jaw or the crotch of the opponent. The basic movements: Draw the spear with the right hand, slip the hand on the butt and raise the butt forward and upward from below, with the power focused on the end of the butt. (Fig. 2-70, 2-71, 2-72) Raise the butt with the high stance or the low stance, depending on the situation.

Butt slamming is used in the same situation as spear slamming. Technically, it is similar to the cut. The basic movements: Slam the spear downward to the ground from above with one or both hands. (Fig. 2-73, 2-74)

Fig. 2-66

Fig. 2-67

Fig. 2-68

Fig. 2-69

Fig. 2-70

47

Fig. 2-71

Fig. 2-72

48

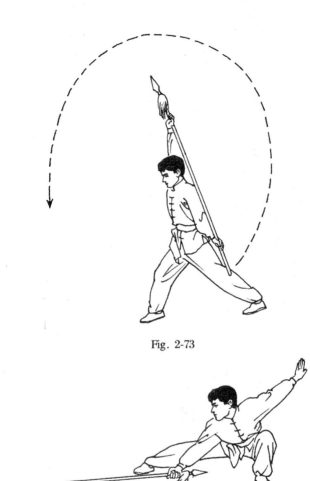

Fig. 2-73

Fig. 2-74

### 17. uppercut

This is an attacking technique used to strike the wrist, lower jaw, and crotch of the opponent from a long distance.

The basic movements: Slip the right hand and grip the

middle and rear of the spear, circle the spearhead with both hands upward and backward, and then raise it upward and forward from below on the right side of the body, power focused on the spearhead. (Fig. 2-75, 2-76, 2-77)

Fig. 2-75

Fig. 2-76

Fig. 2-77

These movements can also be executed on the left side of the body. If both hands are raised when executing the upper-cut, it is called the "rising uppercut." It is a very common move in spear play routines.

**18. other techniques**

There are many spear techniques. Here I have described only the most common and basic techniques, out of which many others have evolved.

There are some techniques which are not considered as important, but are commonly used in routines, such as tossing and receiving, the horizontal block, the overhead block, and pulling and dragging.

Toss and receive: The basic movements: Toss the spear into the air with one or both hands, and receive it after it turns over 180 or 360 degrees. (Fig. 2-78, 2-79, 2-80, 2-81) Taking the spear in behind-the-back piercing is also considered one of the tossing and receiving techniques.

Horizontal block: Hold the spear with one hand and use the other palm to support the shaft. (Fig. 2-82)

Fig. 2-78

Fig. 2-79

Overhead block: Hold the spear overhead with the hands wide apart. (Fig. 2-83)

Pull: Hold the spear in one hand, arm bent, and keep the

Fig. 2-80

Fig. 2-81

53

other hand as wide apart as possible so that the spear lies horizontally in front of the chest and on one side of the body. (Fig. 2-84)

Drag: Feigning defeat to give the opponent a back thrust. The basic movements: Hold the spear in one hand and draw the spearhead behind the body with a walking step or other movements. (Fig. 2-85, 2-86)

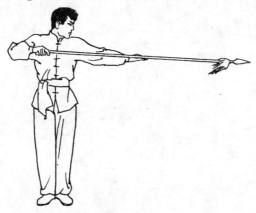

Fig. 2-82

Fig. 2-83

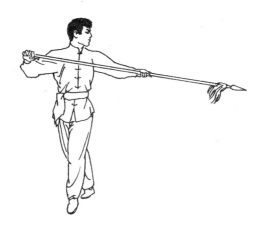

Fig. 2-84

Fig. 2-85

Horizontal thrust with changing grips: This is a technique used for slipping hands and changing grips in some spear play routines. The basic movements: Slip the left hand forward to the front of the spear, change the right hand grip with the radi-

55

al facing the spear butt and thrust the spearhead forward and to the left horizontally. Then slip the right hand to the front of the spear. Change the left hand grip, hold the shaft with the left hand in front of the right hand, and slip it to the spear butt. Change the right hand grip so that the radial faces the spearhead, and thrust it horizontally forward and to the left. Do this exercise repeatedly, as above or with the walking step. (Fig. 2-87, 2-88, 2-89, 2-90)

Fig. 2-86

Fig. 2-87

Fig. 2-88

Fig. 2-89

Fig. 2-90

57

## *Chapter Three*   Basic Skills

The spear should be (1) thrust on a straight line. Spear play is dominated by the thrusting technique, and thrusting the spear on a straight line is the basic requirement of this technique. In thrusting the spear, the movement must be executed like a straight line extending forward, with the power of the entire body focused on the spearhead through the shaft. This makes the thrusting line shorter and the movement quicker and more powerful. The ability to focus power on the spearhead is an important criterion for judging one's mastery of spear-play skills. To achieve this, you must keep the wrist out, extend the shoulders, twist the waist, stretch the rear leg, and stamp the rear foot. Exert the force forward in a straight line. The power release must be quick and soft, and accelerated gradually. When the rear hand approaches the front hand, thrust the spear forward abruptly with an "explosive force", and then retrieve the spear quickly. This is called "going like an arrow and coming like a straight line." In thrusting the spear, you must have complete control of it so that the spear does not move up and down or shake to the left or right. It is also essential to have the tip of the nose, the point of the spearhead, and the toes all on a straight line vertically, with the power of the entire body concentrated on the point of the spearhead so that it will directly find the target with accuracy. And the spear must be kept close to the waist for a powerful thrust. The saying that "the spear is a lock around the waist" means that the end of the spear butt must be lower than the spearhead and close to the waist. The thrust must be executed from the waist so that the spear has a firm support and the power is released

58

from the waist. The recoiled spear must then return to the waist for the next thrust.

(2) You must have correct posture. The basic posture for holding the spear consists of the "four levels." The four levels are a level top, level shoulders, a level spear, and level feet. A level top means keeping the head upright and the neck straight. Only when the head is upright and the neck straight can the player use the spear with full vigor and bright eyes. Level shoulders mean dropping the shoulders and the elbows. Only when the shoulders are level can the body be upright; only when the body is upright can the stance be firm; and only when the stance is firm can the technique be flexible. Level spear means forming a horizontal line between the hands and the point of the spearhead. Only when the spear is kept level can it be used easily for attack or defence and the spear be moved quickly. Level feet mean stepping with both feet fully and solidly on the ground, and not empty. The front foot is not to be raised without a reason, nor is the rear foot move at a whim. Moreover, both legs must be bent when the spear is held in the hands because this helps to lower the body's center of gravity and keep the posture steady.

(3) Spear play should be active. Excellent spear play is not limited only to the strict and forceful execution of one movement or one exercise. In the cut, flick, and parry movements, the spear should be played freely and nimbly, like an undulating dragon. Holding the spear is sometimes called holding the dragon, and the spear is customarily regarded as "dragon." This means that spear play is not rigid, but flexible and diverse. Spear play routines are by no means combinations of single or identical movements, but rather they consist of these movements as well as other turning, rising, and falling movements. This is why spear play should be active, the unity of opposites between the single movements and the overall routine. Therefore, in practising spear play you must not only

59

have good technique, but also the ability to put together entire routines.

(4) Be good at circling. Circling means that the spearhead always moves along a circular or curved line. Many spear techniques are executed with circles. In the outward parry, for example, the spearhead moves around the left semicircle, and around the right semicircle in the inward parry. In the coil, the spearhead moves continuously around a full circle. The circles include left and right semicircles, upper and lower semicircles, and large and small full circles. The semicircle is the curved line and the full circle is the circular line. The circle is the very foundation of spear play.

The circle should not be too big, not bigger than five *chi* (one *chi* is the equivalent of 1/3 meter). When on the side, the range should not be bigger than one *chi*. This is because if the circle is too big the line of movement is too long, making defence too loose and attack too slow. To prevent this, the movement of the spear should not be higher than shoulder level or lower than knee level. The size of the circle should be determined by the situational needs of attack or defense.

## Chapter Four
## Becoming Proficient at Spear Play

Spear play has been called the "king of arts." At first glance, it may appear that spear play movements are not difficult. There is not much turning, tumbling, jumping or acrobatics involved. But in fact it is rather difficult to master spear play. One reason is that spear play calls for clear points of force. That is, the spear must be thrust forward on a straight line with the power focused on the point of the spearhead. The spear must also be played tightly. Whether in the parry or in the coil, you must be good at circling. When the circle is tight, there is nothing that can get into it. At the same time, it must be fully extended. Since the spear is a long-shaft weapon, when techniques change from time to time, the range of movement is wide and the spear rises and falls suddenly. A high degree of coordination is needed to couple the hand techniques with the footwork so the spear is played freely like an undulating dragon. Therefore, in learning spear play you should not begin with the routines or with the complicated techniques, or you will have to go back to the basics all over again.

The first step is to diligently practise the parries and thrusting exercises.

Superficially, the parries and thrusts are not difficult movements. However, it is impossible to execute the parries well if you are not good at circling and making the circles close and tight. You have to practise it diligently. It is even more difficult to achieve the "four levels," that is, form a vertical line along the tip of the nose, the point of the spearhead and

61

the toes while focusing the power on the spearhead while thrusting. Therefore, it is essential to practise the parries and thrusts. You must persist in practising the parries and thrusts even after you have learned the routines and attained a high level of play.

In learning to play the spear, you have to stand in the bow stance like a good archer. The movements of the hands, waist and legs should be well coordinated. Don't be afraid of pains and soreness, and remember: practice makes perfect. A good method is to divide the exercises into sets of repetitions. For example, you can repeat the same exercise 20 times in one set, and practise five different sets. As your skills improve, you can do 30 or even 40 repitions in one set and practise eight or ten different sets.

Of course, sometimes you can also practise a mixture of movements. For example, you may first do one or two sets of parries and thrusts, then a set of figures, and do them alternately.

When you find yourself becoming good at the parries and thrusts, go on to learn the other techniques.

The second step is to learn the other spear techniques. There are strict requirements for the grip, force exertion, and force points for each technique. Every movement must be practised repeatedly until you have a clear understanding of spear play. You can practise figures, the coil, cloud floating, the upward parry and piercing in sets, and repeat them several times. As for cutting, pointing, raising and flicking, you can practice these in mixtures. For example, practise pointing with flicking, and cutting with rising.

The third step is to grasp the connections and transitions between different techniques. The figures, the rising uppercut, cloud floating spear, and swinging exercises all must be done skillfully and freely. Changes of techniques throughout play call for free movement of the spear when slipping hands,

62

changing grips, and taking steps. The front hand must be nimble, the spear must be held nimbly while taking steps, and the point of the spearhead must always move in circles. The grip must not be stiff when moving.

Besides, in tossing and receiving the spear, the overhead block, withdrawing the spear or holding the spear, there are certain requirements. Once you have learned these techniques you can start the combination exercises.

The fourth step is to become skilled at performing the combination exercises. The combination exercises help you to connect different spear techniques closely and harmoniously, coordinate the body movements and the spear movements, and understand the rhythmic changes as the movements are connected. At the beginning, the connections should be executed slowly. After you have a clear idea of the lines of movement and the force points you can do them faster.

The fifth step is to learn the overall routines. Learn them slowly at first, and then more rapidly. From the beginning you should strive for accuracy in the execution of the movements to ensure that the line of movement is clear, the technique is correct, and the force is exerted precisely. Try to understand the cooperation between the footwork and the body techniques, and between the spear techniques and the body techniques in the course of practice, and then gradually increase the speed and strengthen the sense of rhythm. In the repetitions, do your best to understand when the slow movements should change to quick movements, when the quick movements should be connected with other quick movements, the proper cadence, and when the movements should be suspended to display the posture.

In learning the routines, begin part by part, you don't need to hurry through the whole routine. After you become good at the first part, go on with the second part.

When the entire routine is learned you should make full use of the technique of thinking in images. Thinking in images is just like watching a film. Think over and visualize how the rhythms and spirit should be conveyed when executing the movements. Only by combining all the movements of the routine to form an integral and artistic whole is it possible to exhibit spear play as a majestic and lively art.

Of course, attention also must be paid to the technical side of spear play. The spear should not be played like the cudgel, otherwise, though the play is lively, the power cannot be focused on the point of the spearhead. Spear play is exquisite. The movements change in a great variety of directions and over a wide range.

A final point should be made that the basic body movements and standards in modern spear play routines are the same as those in long-style boxing. The footwork, stances, jumps and leg techniques also are all based on the basic techniques and skills of long-style boxing. If you are a beginner and know nothing about Wushu, it would be best if you first learned long-style boxing and then went on to learn spear play on that basis.

# *Chapter Five* Routines

The Movements
Hold Spear with Feet Together
Opening Form

## Part One

I. Lower Thrust with Feet Together
II. Upper Lift with One Hand and Bow Step
III. Hold Spear with Seated Step
IV. Withdraw Spear with Circular Walking Step
V. Point with Jump
VI. Lower Push with Bow Step
VII. Lower Parry with Back Cross Step
VIII. Horizontal Push with Bow Step
IX. Upper Inward Parry with Feet Together and Body Turn
X. Raise Spear Butt with Forward Step and Legs Crossed Backward
XI. Parry Outward and Inward with Half Body Turn, and Thrust with Bow Step

## Part Two

I. Left and Right Figures with Forward Step
II. Shoulder Spear with Back Cross Step
III. Across-the-Back Spear with Waist Turn
IV. Lower Thrust with Body Roll, Jump, Leap, and Cross-Legged Sitting

V. Cloud Spear and Parries with Crossed Legs, and Thrust with Bow Step

## Part Three

I. Spear Butt Uppercut with Body Bending Backward
II. Bump Downward with Seated Stance
III. Cut with Spear Butt, Body Turned and Crouched
IV. Toss and Receive, Hold Spear with Half Body Turn
V. Parry Inward with Backward Step and Body Turn, Lower Thrust with Back Cross Step
VI. Parry Outward and Cut with Forward Step
VII. Cut with Half Body Turn and Toe Step
VIII. Flick with Jump, Half Body Turn and Seated Stance

## Part Four

I. Low-Stance Press with Crouch
II. Parry Outward and Inward, and Thrust with Bow Step
III. Parry Outward and Inward with Forward Step, and Thrust with Jump and Snap Kick
IV. Raise Spear Butt with Bow Step
V. Left and Right Figures
VI. Figures with Forward Steps, and Lower Thrust with Jump and Half Body Turn
VII. Hold Spear with Swinging, Sweeping, Body Turn, and Empty Step

## Part Five

I. Raise Spear Upward and Parry Downward with Circular Walking Step
II. Point with Front Cross Step and Waist Turn

III. Parry Inward and Thrust with Bow Step
IV. Parry Outward and Inward with Leap, and Thrust with Bow Step
V. Spear Butt Lift with Forward Step, and Downward Jab with Cross Step

## Part Six

I. Uppercut and Thrust with Body Bending Backward
II. Parry Inward and Thrust with Legs Crossed and Body Turn
III. Pierce with Backward Step, Body Turn and Trunk Circling
IV. Pierce Around Throat
V. Left and Right Parries with Back Cross Step
VI. Raise Spear Upward with Circular Walking Step, and Point with Legs Crossed
VII. One Hand Upper Thrust with Bow Step
VIII. Withdraw Spear with Backward Step
Closing Form

## Opening Form

Hold the spear with feet together. Hold the spear with the right hand and stand with feet together, spear standing vertically on the right side and eyes looking straight ahead. (Fig. 5-1)

## Part One

### I. Lower Thrust with Feet Together
1. Pivot on the ball of the right foot and the heel of the left foot and turn the body to the left. At the same time, raise the spear slightly with the right hand, and hold the spear with the left hand. (Fig. 5-2)
2. Move the right foot forward and together with the left

Fig. 5-1                    Fig. 5-2

foot. At the same time, drop the spearhead forward and push it forward and downward forcefully with the right hand when it is lowered to waist level to thrust the spearhead downward. Withdraw the left hand to the inner side of the right wrist. (Fig. 5-3)

## II. Upper Lift with One Hand and Bow Step

1. Keep the feet together, draw the spear with the right hand, slip the left hand to the middle of the shaft to circle the spearhead horizontally from forward to the left, backward, and downward. The eyes follow the movement of the spearhead. (Fig. 5-4)

Fig. 5-3

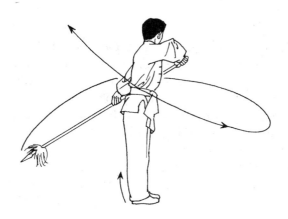

Fig. 5-4

69

2. Raise the right foot to behind the left knee, hold the spear with both hands as their combined force (the right hand moves from the right, past the chest to the left and forward, and the left hand moves from the left forward, to the right and backward around the face) circles the spearhead clockwise over the head, and bend the trunk backward. (Fig. 5-5)

3. Move the right foot backward to the right to form the left bow step, and continue to circle the spearhead from behind to the left. Withdraw the right hand to the right side of the waist, and hold the spear with the left hand. (Fig. 5-6)

Fig. 5-5

4. Continue from the above movement. Hold the shaft with the left hand and move it past the front to above the right shoulder, eyes looking ahead and to the right. Then hold the spear with the right hand to thrust upward to the right, and withdraw the left hand to before the left hip with a pressed palm, and at the same time turn the head to the left, eyes looking ahead and to the left. (Fig. 5-7)

### III. Hold Spear with Seated Step

Raise the right foot and land it behind the left foot to form the seated stance. At the same time, hold the spear butt with the right hand and drop it to the left side of the waist, holding the middle of the shaft with the left hand. (Fig. 5-8)

Fig. 5-6

Fig. 5-7

71

Fig. 5-8

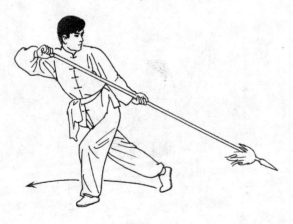

Fig. 5-9

## IV. Withdraw Spear with Circular Walking Step

1. Stand up. Hold the spear with the right hand and raise it in front of the right chest, then hold the spear with the left hand on the left side of the body so that the spearhead drops down behind to the left, eyes on the spearhead. (Fig. 5-9)

2. Hold the spear in the same way, and walk circularly six steps to the back right side, beginning with the right foot. (Fig. 5-10, 5-11, 5-12, 5-13, 5-14, 5-15)

Fig. 5-10

Fig. 5-11

73

Fig. 5-12

Fig. 5-13

Fig. 5-14

Fig. 5-15

75

## V. Point with Jump

1. Move the right foot another step forward. Hold the spear butt with the right hand and send it forward slightly to the left side, and move the left hand from the left side to the right with the spearhead in front of the body. (Fig. 5-16)

2. Raise the left foot upward and forward, bend the right leg behind the left leg after stamping the right foot. At the same time, circle the left hand in front of the body, to the right and upward, so that the spearhead circles upward. Raise the right hand quickly and press the left hand downward while jumping into the air so that the spearhead points downward forcefully. (Fig. 5-17)

## VI. Lower Push with Bow Step

1. When the left foot lands, raise the spear upward and backward. (Fig. 5-18)

2. Land the right foot forward to the right to form the right bow step. At the same time, circle the spear to the left, downward, to the right, then forward and downward. Hold the spear butt with the right hand and turn the wrist over above the right shoulder. Push the spear to the right with the left hand, with the force focused on the front of the shaft. (Fig. 5-19)

## VII. Lower Parry with Back Cross Step

1. Keep the same stance, and circle the spear overhead to the left, with the left palm supporting the shaft. (Fig. 5-20)

2. Continue to circle the shaft from the left side backward, and to the right forward to the front of the chest, eyes on the spearhead. (Fig. 5-21)

3. Move the right foot backward to behind the left side of the left foot to form the cross step. At the same time, hold the shaft with the left hand so that the spearhead continues to parry to the right, downward, and past in the front of the body downward to the left. (Fig. 5-22)

Fig. 5-16

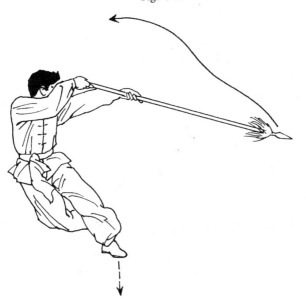

Fig. 5-17

Fig. 5-18

Fig. 5-19

Fig. 5-20

Fig. 5-21

Fig. 5-22

## VIII. Horizontal Push with Bow Step

1. Keep the same stance, raise the trunk and shift the body weight to the left foot. Hold the shaft with the left hand, and circle the spearhead from the left side of the body forward, to the right upward, to the left and overhead and to the left backward, with the left palm supporting the shaft, eyes following the spearhead. (Fig. 5-23)

2. Move the right foot to the right and turn the body 90 degrees to the right to form the right bow step. At the same time, hold the spear butt with the right hand and withdraw it to above the right shoulder. Hold the shaft with the left hand to push it horizontally from left to right, with the power focused on the front of the shaft. (Fig. 5-24)

## IX. Upper Inward Parry with Feet Together and Body Turn

1. Withdraw the right foot to the left foot and put the feet together. Hold the shaft with the left hand to parry outward, to the left backward and downward. Keep the shaft obliquely

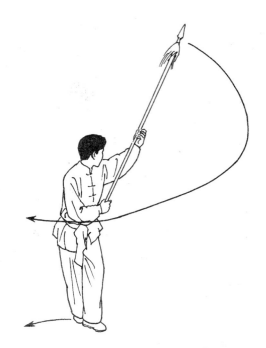

Fig. 5-23

Fig. 5-24

81

close to the chest and turn the body immediately to the left one and a half revolutions, with the spear circling simultaneously. (Fig. 5-25, 5-26)

Fig. 5-25

Fig. 5-26

2. Move the left foot forward to the left side to form the semi-horse-riding step. Hold the spear butt with the right hand and withdraw it to the right side of the waist (palm inward). Hold the shaft with the left hand and turn the wrist from the left upward and to the right downward (palm downward) to move the spearhead in a 30 cm circle for an inward parry. (Fig. 5-27)

3. Shift the body weight forward to form the left bow step. Hold the spear butt with the right hand and send it straight forward so that the spearhead thrusts straight forward. Slip the left hand backward to the radial of the right hand to help hold the spear butt for the thrust. (Fig. 5-28)

Fig. 5-27

Fig. 5-28

## X. Raise Spear Butt with Forward Step and Legs Crossed Backward

1. Keep the same stance. Pull the shaft straight backward with the right hand to the right side of the waist, and slip the left hand forward behind the spearhead. (Fig. 5-29)

2. Move the right foot forward and place the instep against the back side of the left knee. At the same time, slip the right hand to the middle of the shaft and raise the spear butt forward from the right side of the body, with the force focused on the spear butt. Hold the spear with the left hand and withdraw it to the left side of the waist, eyes on the spear butt. (Fig. 5-30)

## XI. Parry Outward and Inward with Half Body Turn, and Thrust with Bow Step

1. Land the left foot backward and turn the body 90 degrees backward to the left. At the same time, hold the spear with the left hand and pull it backward by the left side of the waist. Slip the right hand backward to the butt end and withdraw it to the waist. Slip the left hand to the middle of the shaft. Turn both wrists outward so that the spearhead moves counterclockwise around a 30 cm circle to parry outward. (Fig. 5-31)

2. Turn the left tiptoes outward, turn the trunk 90 degrees to the left, and shift the body weight slightly forward to form the semi-horse-riding step to execute the inward parry. (Fig. 5-32)

3. Shift the body weight forward to form the left bow step to execute the horizontal thrust forward. (Fig. 5-33)

Fig. 5-29

Fig. 5-30

85

Fig. 5-31

Fig. 5-32

Fig. 5-33

## Part Two

### I. Left and Right Figures with Forward Step

1. Move the left foot half a step backward. At the same time, hold the spear butt with the right hand and pull it backward to the right side of the waist. Slip the left hand to the 1/3 of the shaft front and slip the right hand to the 1/3 of the shaft rear. (Fig. 5-34)

2. Move the right foot a small step forward. At the same time, use both hands to move the spear in figures outside the left foot, the spearhead circling from outside the left ankle backward, upward, and forward to form a vertical circle, and the spear butt circling from behind the body, upward, forward, and to the left downward to behind the body. (Fig. 5-35)

3. Move the left foot a small step forward. At the same time, use both hands to move the spear in figures outside the right leg, the spearhead circling from outside the right ankle backward, upward, forward, and downward to form a vertical circle, and the spear butt circling backward, upward, forward, and downward to the right side, backward and upward. (Fig. 5-36)

4. Move the right foot a small step forward, and use both hands to move the spear in figures to the left side of the body (the same as in the second paragraph). (fig. 5-37)

Fig. 5-34

Fig. 5-35

Fig. 5-36

Fig. 5-37

## II. Shoulder Spear with Back Cross Step

1. Extend the right foot outward. Hold the spear with both hands and circle it in figures on the right side of the body. At the same time, slip both hands to the middle of the shaft. (Fig. 5-38)

2. Continue from the above movement. Move the left foot one step forward, turn the body 90 degrees to the left, and immediately move the right foot backward to the left side of the left foot. At the same time, move the spear in figures in front of the body so that the spearhead continues to move around to the right, upward, to the left, and to above the left shoulder. (Fig. 5-39)

3. Continue from the above movement. Hold the middle of the shaft with both hands to circle the spearhead from below backward, upward, and to the left, then immediately slip the hands to the two ends of the shaft to place the shaft horizontally in front of the chest. (Fig. 5-40)

4. Keep the same stance. Lift the shaft overhead with both hands and place it horizontally on the shoulders. (Fig. 5-41)

## III. Across-the-Back Spear with Waist Turn

1. Shoulder the spear in the same position as above and rotate the waist 180 degrees to the right, with the spear moving 180 degrees around a vertical cycle. (Fig. 5-42)

2. Turn the trunk 90 degrees to the right, the shaft moving from behind the head to the right shoulder to turn the spearhead upward from left to right above the head and in front of the body. (Fig. 5-43)

## IV. Lower Thrust with Body Roll, Jump, Leap, and Cross-Legged Sitting

1. Move the left foot one step forward and hold the shaft with the left hand slightly down to place the shaft obliquely in

Fig. 5-38

Fig. 5-39

91

Fig. 5-40

Fig. 5-41

front of the chest. (Fig. 5-44)

2. Move the right foot a step forward, turn the body 90 degrees to the left, and circle the spearhead around in front of the body from below, past the left shank and to the left. (Fig. 5-45)

3. Stamp the right foot on the ground and turn the body 180 degrees. Jump in a big stride with the left foot forward,

Fig. 5-42

Fig. 5-43

93

Fig. 5-44

Fig. 5-45

the spearhead circling upward, backward, and downward. (Fig. 5-46)

4. Land the left foot first, jump and continue to turn the body 180 degrees with the spear in front of the chest and the spearhead circling to the left, backward and downward on the left side. (Fig. 5-47)

Fig. 5-46

Fig. 5-47

5. Land the right foot behind the left foot and turn the trunk 90 degrees to the left to form the seated stance, and hold the spear butt tightly with both hands to thrust downward, eyes on the spearhead. (Fig. 5-48)

**V. Cloud Spear and Parries with Crossed Legs, and Thrust with Bow Step**

1. Stand up and move the left foot one step forward. At the same time, hold the spear butt with the right hand, elbow

Fig. 5-48

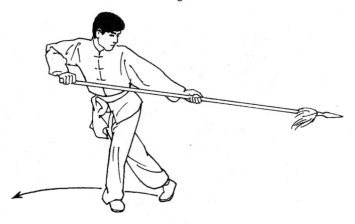

Fig. 5-49

bent, and pull the spear backward in front of the chest, and turn the body 90 degrees to the left so the spearhead points slightly to the left. Hold the middle of the spear with the left hand. (Fig. 5-49)

2. Place the left foot against the inner side of the right knee, hold the spear with both hands to circle it like a cloud over the chest-high horizontal plane from the left forward, to the right, and backward. (Fig. 5-50)

3. Continue to circle the spearhead from behind to the left and to the front of the body, and land the right foot forward to parry outward (Fig. 5-51) and parry inward. (Fig. 5-52)

4. Shift the body weight forward to form the left bow step and thrust the spear straight forward horizontally. (Fig. 5-53)

Fig. 5-50

Fig. 5-51

Fig. 5-52

Fig. 5-53

## Part Three

### I. Spear Butt Uppercut with Body Bending Backward

1. Move the right foot slightly backward. At the same time, hold the spear butt with the right hand and pull it backward along the right side of the waist, and slip the left hand to near the spearhead. (Fig. 5-54)

2. Hold the spear with the left hand and pull it back toward the face. Hold the spear near the head with the right hand and lift the spear butt from behind, forward and upward. At the same time, kick forward with the right foot, body bending backward. (Fig. 5-55)

### II. Bump Downward with Seated Stance

1. Land the right foot backward and raise the body. At the same time, change to the left hand grip and hold the spear in front of the right hand, radial toward the spear butt. Change to the right hand grip and hold the spear by the head, eyes looking back to the lower right. (Fig. 5-56)

2. Move the left foot one step backward and squat down to form the cross-legged stance. At the same time, hold the spearhead with the right hand to bump it backward and downward to the right. Slip the left hand to the spear butt, eyes on the spearhead. (Fig. 5-57)

### III. Cut with Spear Butt, Body Turned and Crouched

1. Rise up to a half squat, turn the waist slightly upward to the left. At the same time, hold the spear with the right hand, lift it overhead, and shoulder it on the back, eyes on the spearhead. (Fig. 5-58)

2. Turn the waist 180 degrees to the left and upward,

Fig. 5-54

Fig. 5-55

spear circling with the body turn and spearhead moving around in a semicircle in front of the body downward, and to the left and upward. (Fig. 5-59)

3. Continue to turn the waist 180 degrees to the left and downward, and at the same time move the right foot one step forward to the left to form the right crouch stance. While turning the body, loosen the grip and change the left hand to a palm, move it from behind the body downward, to the right and upward, and extend it to the upper left, arm straight. Hold the spearhead with the right hand and circle the spear upward, and to the left and downward while turning the body so that the shaft cuts the ground horizontally, eyes on the spear butt. (Fig. 5-60)

Fig. 5-56

Fig. 5-57

Fig. 5-58

Fig. 5-59

Fig. 5-60

## IV. Toss and Receive, Hold Spear with Half Body Turn

1. Shift the body weight to the right to form the right bow step. Hold the spear near the head with the right hand, spear off the ground. (Fig. 5-61) Hold the spear with the right hand to toss it up, spearhead up and shaft rolling forward into the air. Stand up, with the hands ready to receive the spear. (Fig. 5-62)

2. Catch the spear with both hands. Hold the spear butt with the right hand and use the left hand to hold the shaft near the middle. At the same time, move the right foot one step backward to the right. (Fig. 5-63) Turn the body to the right and circle the spearhead in one rotation horizontally from left to right. Shift the body weight to the right foot and hold the spear with the right hand by the right side of the waist. Hold the spear with the left hand and turn it inward, eyes looking ahead. (Fig. 5-64)

## V. Parry Inward with Backward Step and Body Turn, Lower Thrust with Back Cross Step

1. Keep the stance. Hold the spear butt with the right hand, and turn the wrist upward and outward, elbow bent in front of the right side of the chest. Hold the shaft with the left hand to drop the spearhead downward to the left. (Fig. 5-65)

2. Move the right foot backward to behind the left foot and hold the spear with both hands to circle the spearhead from below to the left and backward. (Fig. 5-66)

3. Move the left foot backward to the left and turn the body 45 degrees to the left to form the semi-horse-riding stance. At the same time, execute the inward parry. (Fig. 5-67)

4. Move the right foot backward to behind the left foot to form the cross-legged stance and at the same time thrust the spear backward and downward to the left with both hands. (Fig. 5-68)

Fig. 5-61

Fig. 5-62

Fig. 5-63

Fig. 5-64

Fig. 5-65

Fig. 5-66

107

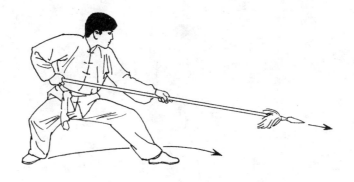

Fig. 5-67

Fig. 5-68

## VI. Parry Outward and Cut with Forward Step

1. Move the right foot forward to the right and stand with feet apart. Hold the spear butt with the right hand to pull the spear backward. Hold the shaft with the left hand and lift it overhead. Turn the wrists to parry outward above the head to the left. (Fig. 5-69)

2. Follow immediately the above movement. Turn the trunk 45 degrees to the right. At the same time, hold the spear with both hands to cut forward from left to right, power focused on the front of the shaft. (Fig. 5-70)

## VII. Cut with Half Body Turn and Toe Step

1. Move the right foot backward to behind the left foot. At the same time, hold the spear with both hands and circle the spearhead from above to the left and backward, eyes on the spearhead. (Fig. 5-71)

2. Continue from the previous movement and move the left foot forward. At the same time, hold the spear with both hands and continue to circle the spearhead from above to the left, backward and downward. (Fig. 5-72)

3. Continue from the previous movement and move the right foot a big step forward. Hold the spear with both hands and lift the spearhead up from the left and behind. (Fig. 5-73)

4. Move the left foot forward to the inner side of the right foot. At the same time, hold the spear with both hands to cut forward and downward from above. Hold the spear butt with the right hand and withdraw it to the right side of the body, power focused on the front of the shaft. (Fig. 5-74)

## VIII. Flick with Jump, Half Body Turn and Seated Stance

1. Move the left foot one step forward to the right and turn the body to the left. At the same time, hold the spear butt with the right hand in front of the chest and turn the spearhead to the

Fig. 5-69

Fig. 5-70

Fig. 5-71

Fig. 5-72

111

Fig. 5-73

Fig. 5-74

right with the left hand, circle it horizontally from above in front of the body to the left and to above and behind the body, eyes on the spearhead. (Fig. 5-75)

2. Stamp the left foot on the ground, leap forward to the right with the right foot, and turn the body 45 degrees to the left and backward while jumping into the air. At the same time, hold the spear near the butt end with the left hand and raise it upward to point the spearhead downward, power focused on the spearhead. (Fig. 5-76)

3. Land the right foot, then land the left foot behind the right foot and squat down to form the seated stance. At the same time, hold the spear butt with the right hand and pull it backward to the right side of the waist so the spearhead retreats upward and backward. Slip the left hand forward to near the middle of the shaft and seize the shaft by an abrupt force with a wrist turn, thus executing the flick. (Fig. 5-77)

## Part Four

### I. Low-Stance Press with Crouch

1. Stand on the right leg, slightly bent, and place the left foot against the back of the right knee. At the same time, hold the spear with both hands to circle it downward to the left, and upward in front of the body. (Fig. 5-78)

2. Land the left foot forward to form the left crouch. At the same time, hold the spear with both hands and continue to circle the spearhead to the right to the front of the body, and press it to the ground forcefully so that the spear lies flat on the ground, eyes on the front of the spear. (Fig. 5-79)

### II. Parry Outward and Inward, and Thrust with Bow Step

1. Raise the body slightly, right leg half bent, and hold the spear with both hands to execute the outward parry forward.

113

Fig. 5-75

Fig. 5-76

114

Fig. 5-77

Fig. 5-78

Fig. 5-79

115

(Fig. 5-80)

2. Shift the body weight slightly forward to form the semi-horse-riding stance to execute the inward parry forward. (Fig. 5-81)

3. Shift the body weight forward to form the left bow step to execute the horizontal thrust forward. (Fig. 5-82)

### III. Parry Outward and Inward with Forward Step, and Thrust with Jump and Snap Kick

1. Raise the body slightly, shift the body weight backward, and hold the spear with both hands to execute the outward parry in front of the body. (Fig. 5-83)

2. Move the right foot one step forward, lower the body weight slightly, hold the spear with both hands to execute the inward parry in front of the body and get ready to jump. (Fig. 5-84)

3. Stamp the right foot on the ground, raise the left knee forward and upward, and hold the spear with both hands to execute the horizontal thrust forward. (Fig. 5-85)

4. Jump and kick forward with the right foot. At the same time, hold the spear butt with the right hand, pull the spear backward to the right side of the waist, slip the left hand to near the spearhead, and slip the right hand from the spear butt to the middle of the shaft. (Fig. 5-86)

### IV. Raise Spear Butt with Bow Step

After landing the left foot, land the right foot forward to form the right bow step. At the same time, hold the spear at the middle with the right hand to raise the spear butt forward and upward to eyebrow level from behind on the right side of the body, power focused on the front end of the spear butt. Hold the shaft near the spearhead with the left hand to circle the spearhead from in front of the body upward, to the left side backward, and downward to the left side of the waist, eyes on the

116

Fig. 5-80

Fig. 5-81

Fig. 5-82

117

Fig. 5-83

Fig. 5-84

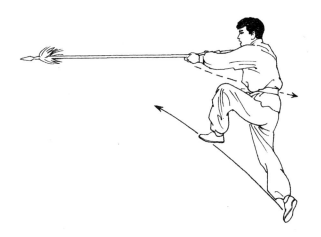

Fig. 5-85

Fig. 5-86

119

spear butt. (Fig. 5-87)

## V. Left and Right Figures

1. Shift the body weight backward to the left foot and move the right foot half a step backward to form the right toe step. Hold the spear with both hands to circle the spearhead upward and forward from the rear. (Fig. 5-88)

2. Shift the body weight forward to the right foot, slip the left hand to the middle of the shaft, hold the spear with both hands to continue to circle the spearhead forward and downward to the outer side of the right leg, and at the same time, turn the trunk to the right side. (Fig. 5-89)

3. Keep the stance. Hold the spear with both hands and continue to circle figures one and a half rotations on the right side so the spear butt moves down on the left side of the body and the spearhead moves forward to above the right shoulder, with the shaft under the right armpit. (Fig. 5-90)

4. Hold the spear with both hands and circle figures one and a half rotations on the left side of the body. While making the last half rotation, move the left foot a step forward so that the spearhead is placed downward from outside the right ankle and the spear butt is above the left shoulder. (Fig. 5-91)

5. Hold the spear with both hands and circle figures one and a half rotations on the right side of the body. While completing the last half rotation, extend the left toes outward and turn the trunk to the left so that the spear butt moves down behind the body on the left side from outside the left foot, and the spearhead is above the right shoulder. (Fig. 5-92)

## VI. Figures with Forward Steps, and Lower Thrust with Jump and Half Body Turn

1. Hold the spear with both hands to circle figures one and a half rotations on the left side of the body. While doing the last half turn, move the right foot a step forward, toes outward, and

120

Fig. 5-87

Fig. 5-88

121

Fig. 5-89

Fig. 5-90

Fig. 5-91

Fig. 5-92

123

move the spearhead down from outside the right foot. (Fig. 5-93)

2. Move the left foot one step forward, and hold the spear with both hands to continue to circle figures on the right side of the body so the spearhead circles from below, backward and forward to the front of the body. Slip the right hand backward to the spear butt end and slip the left hand toward the spearhead, arms fully extended so that they gradually form a straight line with the shaft, lying obliquely in front of the chest. (Fig. 5-94)

3. Stamp the left foot on the ground and stride forward with the right foot raised. Turn the body 180 degrees upward to the left while jumping, raise the left knee, hold the spear butt with the right hand to thrust forward and downward, and change the left hand into a palm and flash it backward and upward, wrist bent. (Fig. 5-95 A, B)

4. Land the right foot, left knee bent, to thrust downward, eyes on the spearhead. (Fig. 5-96)

### VII. Hold Spear with Swinging, Sweeping, Body Turn, and Empty Step

1. Land the left foot backward, slip the left hand to near the radial of the right hand. (Fig. 5-97)

2. Turn the body to the left one and a half rotations, and move both feet one step forward as the body turns. At the same time, hold the spear butt with both hands to sweep the spear around one and a half rotations. (Fig. 5-98)

3. Move the left foot forward to the left, and continue to sweep the spear on a horizontal plane overhead so that the spearhead circles to behind the body, shaft on the right shoulder. (Fig. 5-99)

4. Shift the body weight to the right foot, and move the left foot in front of the right foot to form the left toe step. Hold the spear with both hands and continue to circle the spearhead from behind to the right, in front of the body, to the left, and

Fig. 5-93

Fig. 5-94

125

Fig. 5-95A

Fig. 5-95B

Fig. 5-96

Fig. 5-97

127

Fig. 5-98

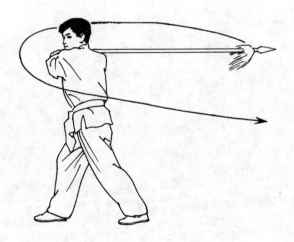

Fig. 5-99

128

backward and downward to behind the body. Hold the spear butt with the right hand, elbow bent, in front of the chest and slip the left hand to the middle of the shaft, eyes looking ahead and to the left. (Fig. 5-100)

Fig. 5-100

## Part Five

### I. Raise Spear Upward and Parry Downward with Circular Walking Step

1. Move the left foot half a step forward to the right, tiptoe outward, shift the body weight forward, loosen the left grip and slip the left hand slightly toward the spearhead, eyes on the spearhead. (Fig. 5-101)

2. Continue from the previous movement, and move the right foot one step forward. At the same time, hold the spear with both hands to raise the spearhead forward and upward to the right along the left side of the body, power focused on the front of the spear. (Fig. 5-102)

3. Move the left foot forward and land it on the right side

Fig. 5-101

Fig. 5-102

of the right foot, tiptoe outward. At the same time, hold the spear with both hands to parry and sweep from right to left, downward and backward, power focused on the front of the shaft. (Fig. 5-103)

## II. Point with Front Cross Step and Waist Turn
1. Continue from the previous movement. Raise the right foot, move it past the left foot and land it before and outside the left foot with toes on the ground. Immediately, bend the trunk forward and turn the waist counterclockwise one rotation. At the same time, hold the spear with both hands and continue to point the spear from behind to upward and forward. Slip the left hand backward to near the spear butt. (Fig. 5-104, 5-105)

## III. Parry Inward and Thrust with Bow Step
1. Stand firmly on the right foot and slip the left hand to near the middle of the shaft. (Fig. 5-106)
2. Move the left foot half a step forward and lower the body weight to form the semi-horse-riding stance. At the same time, hold the spear with the right hand, lower it and withdraw it to the waist. Hold the spear with the left hand, lower it and turn it inward to parry inward. (Fig. 5-107)
3. Shift the body weight forward to form the left bow step, and hold the spear with both hands to thrust forward horizontally. (Fig. 5-108)

## IV. Parry Outward and Inward with Leap, and Thrust with Bow Step
1. Stamp the left foot on the ground and raise the right foot to leap forward in front of the left knee. At the same time, pull the spear butt back with the right hand to parry outward. (Fig. 5-109)
2. Land the right foot and bend the knee to a half squat. Bend the left knee and place it against the back side of the right

Fig. 5-103

Fig. 5-104

Fig. 5-105

Fig. 5-106

133

Fig. 5-107

Fig. 5-108

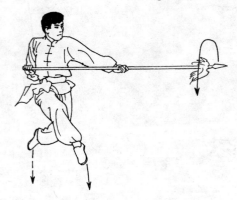

Fig. 5-109

134

knee to parry inward. (Fig. 5-110)

3. Land the left foot forward to form the left bow step and thrust horizontally forward. (Fig. 5-111)

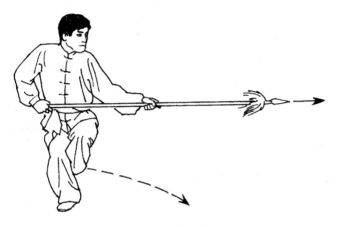

Fig. 5-110

Fig. 5-111

## V. Spear Butt Lift with Forward Step, and Downward Jab with Cross Step

1. Move the right foot slightly forward and raise the body slightly. At the same time, hold the spear butt with the right hand and pull the spear backward and downward along the right side of the waist. Slip the left hand to near the spearhead and slip the right hand 1/3 down to the shaft. (Fig. 5-112)

2. Move the left foot one large step forward and turn the body 90 degrees to the left. Immediately hold the spear with both hands to raise the spear butt forward and upward along the right side of the body, and immediately slip the right hand to the spearhead. (Fig. 5-113)

3. Move the left foot one large step backward to behind the outer side of the right foot to form the cross-legged stance. At the same time, hold the spear near spearhead with the right hand to bump it downward to the right from above in front of the body, and slip the left hand to near the spear butt, eyes on the spearhead. (Fig. 5-114 A)

## Part Six

### I. Uppercut and Thrust with Body Bending Backward

1. Hold the spear with both hands in the same posture. Move the left foot back and one step forward to the left, eyes looking ahead. (Fig. 5-114 B)

2. Raise the right foot forward and upward, knee bent, to kick forward to waist level, instep flat, and bend the trunk backward. At the same time, hold the spear butt with the left hand to pull it back toward the chest. Hold the shaft near the spear butt with the right hand to lift it downward and forward along the outer side of the right foot, and slip the hand forward to thrust the spearhead forward horizontally. (Fig. 5-115)

Fig. 5-112

Fig. 5-113

Fig. 5-114A

Fig. 5-114B

## II. Parry Inward and Thrust with Legs Crossed and Body Turn

1. Raise the body, land the right foot forward, tiptoe slightly inward to the left, and turn the body 90 degrees backward to the left. At the same time, change the left hand grip and hold the shaft at the middle, and slip the right hand to the butt end so that the spearhead circles from in front of the body to the left and downward. (Fig. 5-116)

2. Place the left foot against the back side of the right knee, pivot on the ball of the right foot and turn the body 180 degrees, the spear circling with the body, to keep the spearhead lower and forward on the left side of the body. (Fig. 5-117) Land the left foot forward to the left to form the semi-horse-riding stance to parry inward. (Fig. 5-118)

3. Shift the body weight forward to form the left bow step and thrust horizontally forward. (Fig. 5-119)

## III. Pierce with Backward Step, Body Turn and Trunk Circling

1. Shift the body weight backward and rise slightly. At the same time, hold the spear butt with the right hand and pull it backward to the right, and slip the left hand immediately to near the spearhead. (Fig. 5-120)

2. Continue to push the spear horizontally to the right with the left hand and loosen the grip. Hold the spear with the right hand only and slip it to near the spearhead. (Fig. 5-121)

3. Move the right foot backward and turn the body 180 degrees to the right. At the same time, hold the spear with the left hand in front of the right hand, palm facing up and radial toward the spear butt. (Fig. 5-122)

4. Shift the body weight to the right to form the right bow step. Lean the trunk forward. At the same time, hold the shaft near the spearhead with the right hand, and pull it backward to the right, close to the abdomen. Slip the left hand to near the

139

Fig. 5-115

Fig. 5-116

140

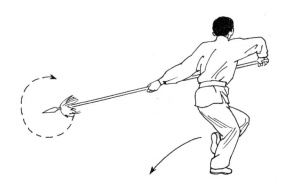

Fig. 5-117

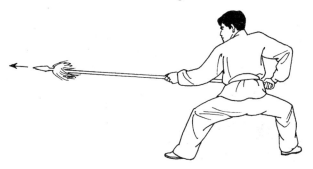

Fig. 5-118

Fig. 5-119

141

Fig. 5-120

Fig. 5-121

142

spear butt, eyes on the spearhead. (Fig. 5-123)

Fig. 5-122

Fig. 5-123

## IV. Pierce Around Throat

1. Keep the stance and raise the body. At the same time, turn the body 90 degrees to the left, hold the spear near the head with the right hand and send it, in front of the abdomen, on a horizontal level to the left, and slip the left hand to near the radial of the right hand. (Fig. 5-124)

2. Bend the trunk backward and bend the right arm to pull the spear to front of the neck. (Fig. 5-125)

3. Keep the stance, and continue to pull the spear in front of the neck to the right on a horizontal level, eyes on the spearhead. (Fig. 5-126)

## V. Left and Right Parries with Back Cross Step

1. Continue from the previous movement. Continue to push the shaft by the throat to the right with the left hand, and loosen the right hand, slip it to the spear butt and hold it tightly again. Turn the body 90 degrees to the right. At the same time, hold spear butt with the right hand and turn it inward, elbow bent, and use the left hand to quickly hold the middle of the shaft. (Fig. 5-127)

2. Move the left foot one step forward to the left side, hold the spear with both hands to parry the front end of the spear at knee level about 40 cm backward, to the left, and slip the left hand slightly downward. (Fig. 5-128)

3. Move the right foot backward to the left side of the left foot. At the same time, push the spear with the left hand to the right and slip the left hand upward to parry the front of the spear from left to right, then immediately parry it back from right to left. (Fig. 5-129)

## VI. Raise Spear Upward with Circular Walking Step, and Point with Legs Crossed

1. Move the left foot forward to the left, tiptoe outward, and turn the trunk 90 degrees to the left. Hold the spear with

Fig. 5-124

Fig. 5-125

145

Fig. 5-126

Fig. 5-127

146

Fig. 5-128

Fig. 5-129

both hands to push the spear backward and downward to the left. (Fig. 5-130)

2. Move the right foot one step forward to the front of the left foot, and hold the spear with both hands to circle the spearhead from below forward, upward and backward. (Fig. 5-131)

3. Move the left foot one step circularly forward to the left from inside the right foot, and turn the trunk 90 degrees to the left. Hold the spear with both hands to circle its head to the left, downward and backward while turning the body, eyes on the spearhead. (Fig. 5-132)

4. Turn the body 90 degrees to the left, move the right foot forward, and move the left foot another step forward. Hold the spear with both hands to raise its head upward from behind the body. (Fig. 5-133 A, 5-133 B)

5. Bend the left leg to a half squat, bend the right leg and place the right foot against the back side of the left knee. Hold the spear with both hands to point its head forward and downward from above, eyes on the head. (Fig. 5-134)

## VII. One Hand Upper Thrust with Bow Step

1. Continue from the previous movement, raise the trunk and pull the spear butt with the right hand in front of the chest. Slip the left hand forward to near the middle of the shaft to raise the spearhead upward and backward above the left shoulder. (Fig. 5-135)

2. Bend the trunk backward, and hold the spear with both hands to circle the spearhead horizontally to the left, forward, and to the right, and the shaft past in front of the body. (Fig. 5-136)

3. Land the right foot backward and raise the trunk to form the left bow step. Hold the spear with both hands to circle the spearhead to the left, forward and in front of the body on the left, and withdraw the right hand to the left side of the waist to hold the spear. (Fig. 5-137)

Fig. 5-130

Fig. 5-131

149

Fig. 5-132

Fig. 5-133A

150

Fig. 5-133B

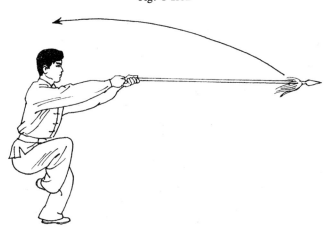

Fig. 5-134

151

Fig. 5-135

Fig. 5-136

152

Fig. 5-137

4. Shift the body weight to the right to form the right bow step. At the same time, hold the spear with the left hand, and push the shaft horizontally to the right and in front of the body so that the spear stands obliquely by the side of the right shoulder. (Fig. 5-138) Hold the spear butt with the right hand and thrust it upward on the right side from the waist, head up, as the left hand leaves the shaft and pushes a horizontal palm forward to the left, eyes looking to the left. (Fig. 5-139)

### VIII. Withdraw Spear with Backward Step
1. Move the right foot one step backward to behind the left foot. Hold the spear butt with the right hand and lower it to the left side of the waist. Take the shaft by the middle with the left hand, above the left shoulder. (Fig. 5-140)
2. Move the left foot one step backward, and continue to

slip the left hand toward the spearhead so as to circle it backward, downward, forward, and outside the left leg. (Fig. 5-141)

3. Land the right foot by the left foot, feet together. Hold the spear with both hands, grip the spear butt with the right hand to circle it backward to the right and downward to the right side of the waist. Hold the shaft with the left hand to move the spearhead forward, past the front of the body to above the right shoulder, and then loosen the grip, and push it to the left with a horizontal push palm, eyes looking ahead and to the left. (Fig. 5-142)

### Closing Form

Drop the left hand down naturally by the left side of the body. Hold the spear with the right hand and stand it vertically by the right side of the body, eyes looking ahead. (Fig. 5-143)

Fig. 5-138

154

Fig. 5-139

Fig. 5-140

155

Fig. 5-141

Fig. 5-142

Fig. 5-143

# Chapter Six   Basic Combination Exercises

**Group One** Hold Spear with Feet Together——Parry Inward, Parry Outward and Thrust with Backward Step——Parry Inward, Parry Outward and Thrust with Back Cross Step——Parry Inward, Parry Outward and Thrust with Leaping Step——Single Hand Lower Thrust with Half Body Turn

1. Stand with feet together, hold the spear with the right hand 1/3 down from the spear butt, arm bent, by the right side of the waist, and place the left palm against the left side of the body. (Fig. 6-1)

2. Move the right foot one half step to the right, turn the trunk 90 degrees to the left, and bend the legs to a half squat to form the semi-horse-riding stance. At the same time, drop the shaft toward the left in front of the body, hold the shaft in the middle with the left hand, and hold the spear butt with the right hand by the right side of the waist. (Fig. 6-2) Use the combined force of the hands, mainly the force of the left hand, to

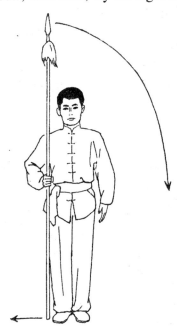

Fig. 6-1

move the front end of the spear to parry outward counterclockwise from below upward, force focused on the front of the shaft. This is called the outward parry. (Fig. 6-3) Shift the body weight slightly forward, use the combined force of the hands, mainly the force of the left hand, to move the front end of the spear to turn and press clockwise from the left upward and to the right, force focused on the front of the shaft. This is called the inward parry. (Fig. 6-4) The diameter of the arc for either the outward or inward parry should not be larger than 40 centimeters. Continue to shift the body weight forward, and straighten the right leg to form the left bow step. Loosen the left hand grip, hold the spear with the right hand and exert the force horizontally to the front, force focused on the spearhead. This is called the thrust. (Fig. 6-5)

3. Raise the body slightly, move the right foot backward to behind the left foot of the left side, turn the trunk slightly to the right, and at the same time, parry outward. (Fig. 6-6) Turn the body slightly to the left and move the left foot one step forward to form the left bow step, and at the same time, parry inward. (Fig. 6-7) Straighten the right leg to form the left bow step and thrust. (Fig. 6-8)

4. Stamp the left foot on the ground, raise the right foot to leap forward, and at the same time parry outward. (Fig. 6-9) Land the feet in order, and at the same time parry inward. (Fig. 6-10) Straighten the right leg to form the left bow step, and at the same time, thrust. (Fig. 6-11)

5. Move the right foot one step forward, pull the spear with the right hand, and slip the left hand forward. (Fig. 6-12) Move the left foot backward to behind the right foot, and at the same time hold the spear with both hands to turn the waist upward and to the left so that the spearhead is raised upward and backward. (Fig. 6-13) Continue to turn the body to the left, move the right foot backward to the right with the leg straightened, and bend the left knee to form the left bow step. Hold the

Fig. 6-2

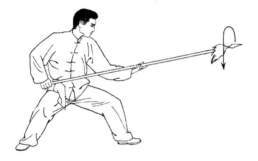

Fig. 6-3

Fig. 6-4

159

Fig. 6-5

Fig. 6-6

Fig. 6-7

160

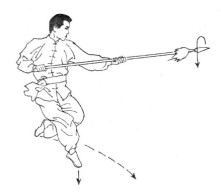

Fig. 6-8

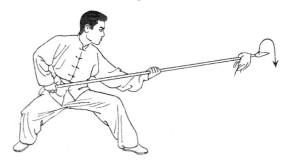

Fig. 6-9

Fig. 6-10

161

Fig. 6-11

Fig. 6-12

162

spear with both hands, and continue to move it downward and to the right. Use the right hand to forcefully thrust the spear forward to the lower-right, take the left hand off and extend it to the upper-rear above the left shoulder. Eyes on the spearhead. (Fig. 6-14)

Fig. 6-13

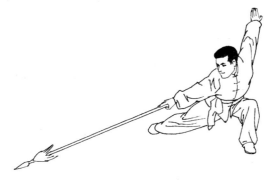

Fig. 6-14

163

**Group Two** Thrust Downward with Feet Together——
Block Spear with Bow Step——Parry Inward with Bow
Step——Parry Inward with Body Turn——Parry Inward with
Semi-Horse-Riding Stance——Thrust with Bow Step

Initial posture: Hold the spear with feet together. (Fig. 6-1)

1. Turn the body 45 degrees to the left with feet together,
lower the spear with the right hand obliquely forward to the left,
and use the left hand to take and hold it in front of the body.
When the spear is lowered to below the knee, use the right hand
to forcefully thrust the spear forward to the lower left, and place
the left palm by the inner side of the right hand, eyes on the
spearhead. (Fig. 6-15)

2. Move the right foot one step to the right side, and bend
the knee to form the right bow step. Pull the spear with the right
hand to the right side, and slip the left hand to the middle of the
shaft to block the spear horizontally forward, above the head.
Eyes looking ahead and to the left. (Fig. 6-16)

3. Keep the stance. Hold the spear with the right hand,
lower it and withdraw it to the waist. At the same time, hold the
spear with the left hand, turn it inward and press it down and
parry inward. Eyes on the spearhead. (Fig. 6-17)

4. Move the left foot to the right foot and put the feet together, immediately turn the body 360 degrees backward to the
left. At the same time, hold the spear with the right hand and
raise it in front of the chest. Slip the left hand forward so that
the spear sweeps and parries to the lower left backward, force
focused on the front of the shaft. Eyes on the front of the shaft.
(Fig. 6-18, 6-19)

5. Move the left foot forward and bend the legs to form
the semi-horse-riding stance. At the same time, hold the spear
with the right hand and withdraw it to the waist. Hold the spear
with the left hand and turn it inward to parry inward. (Fig. 6-20)

Fig. 6-15

Fig. 6-16

165

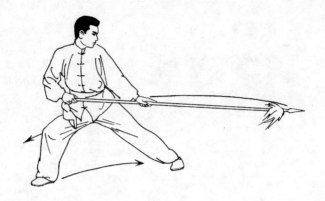

Fig. 6-17

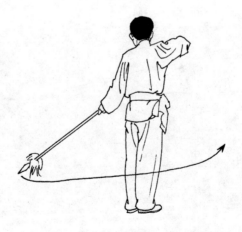

Fig. 6-18

Fig. 6-19

Fig. 6-20

Fig. 6-21

167

6. Straighten the right leg to form the left bow step. At the same time, use the right hand forcefully and loosen the left-hand grip to thrust the spearhead horizontally forward, left hand in front of the right hand. Eyes looking ahead. (Fig. 6-21)

**Group Three** Hold Spear with Semi-Horse-Riding Stance——Coil with Forward Step——Parry Downward with Half Body Turn——Upper Push with Raised Knee

Initial posture: Hold the spear with feet together. (Fig. 6-1)

1. Move the left foot one step forward to the left side, turn the body to the left, and bend both legs to a half squat to form the semi-horse-riding stance. At the same time, lower the spear forward to the left, hold the spear butt with the right hand at the waist, and hold the shaft at the middle with the left hand. Eyes looking ahead. (Fig. 6-22)

2. Move the right foot one step forward, and tiptoe outward. Hold the spear with both hands to circle the spearhead counterclockwise one rotation in a 30 cm diameter. Eyes looking ahead. (Fig. 6-23)

3. Move the left foot and right foot alternately forward, and coil the spear continuously. Move six steps and coil for six rotations. (Fig. 6-24, 6-25)

4. Move the left foot one step forward. At the same time hold the spear with the right hand and turn it inward in front of the chest. Slip the left hand forward to sweep and parry the spear to the lower left, behind the body. Eyes on the front of the spear. (Fig. 6-26)

5. Stand on the left leg and raise the right foot, knee bent. At the same time, hold the spear with both hands and push it forward from behind to the upper right, force focused on the front of the spear. Eyes looking ahead upward. (Fig. 6-27)

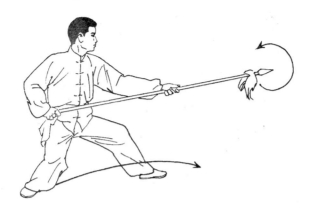

Fig. 6-22

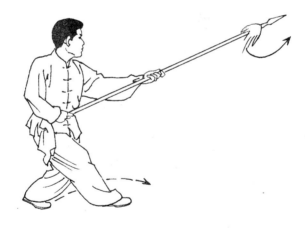

Fig. 6-23

169

Fig. 6-24

Fig. 6-25

170

Fig. 6-26

Fig. 6-27

**Group Four** Hold Spear with Semi-Horse-Riding Stance——
Spear Butt Uppercut with Body Bending Backward and Forward-
Kick——Bumping with Cross Step——Shoulder Spear with
Waist Turn——Spear Butt Slam with Crouch

Initial posture: Hold the spear with feet together. (Fig. 6-
1)

1. Hold the spear while in the semi-horse-riding stance,
the same as in the previous group. (Fig. 6-28)

2. Raise the body slightly, hold the spear butt with the
right hand and pull the spear backward. Slip the left hand forward. (Fig. 6-29) Immediately raise the spear butt from below
forward, slip the left hand to near the spearhead, and hold the
shaft with the right hand near the left hand. At the same time,
bend the trunk backward and kick forward with the right foot,
eyes on the spear butt. (Fig. 6-30)

3. Land the right foot backward, change the grips of both
hands, and hold the shaft near the head with the right hand.
(Fig. 6-31) Immediately, move the left foot backward behind
the right foot to form the cross step. At the same time, hold the
shaft near the spearhead to bump and thrust the spear to the lower right. Slip the left hand 1/3 down from the spear butt, force
focused on the spearhead. Eyes on the front of the spear. (Fig.
6-32)

4. Continue from the previous movement. Shoulder the
spear on the back with both hands and turn the waist to the left
and upward. (Fig. 6-33)

5. Move the left foot one big step backward to the right
side and bend the knees to a full squat to form the right crouch
stance. At the same time, hold the spear with the right hand and
slam the spear butt on the ground from above. Extend the left
hand to the rear upper left with a full palm. Eyes looking downward ahead. (Fig. 6-34, 6-35)

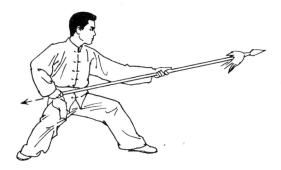

Fig. 6-28

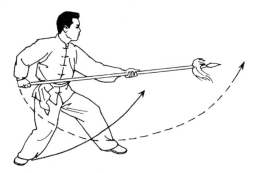

Fig. 6-29

Fig. 6-30

Fig. 6-31

Fig. 6-32

Fig. 6-33

Fig. 6-34

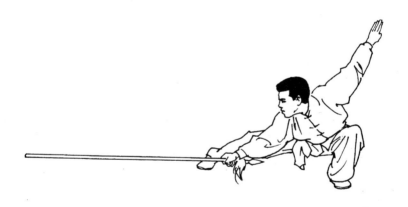

Fig. 6-35

175

**Group Five** Hold Spear with Semi-Horse-Riding Stance——Slip Spear with Backhand Grip——Bump Downward with Body Turn and Bow Step

Initial posture: Hold the spear with feet together. (Fig. 6-1)

1. Hold the spear with both hands while in the semi-horse-riding stance. (Fig. 6-36)

2. Raise the body slightly, hold the spear butt with the right hand and pull the spear backward, radial relaxed, with the palm supporting the butt end. (Fig. 6-37) Loosen the left hand grip. While pushing the spear forward with the right palm, turn the wrist inward counterclockwise and hold the spear butt with the backhand grip, radial toward the butt end. (Fig. 6-38)

3. Loosen the grip after pulling the spear backward to the lower right with the right hand. Use the left hand to forcefully pierce the spear to the lower right, and continue to turn the right hand inward with the back up, and slip the hand to near the spearhead. Take the left hand off after sending the spear forward, and bend the elbow in front of the right shoulder. (Fig. 6-39, 6-40)

4. Move the left foot forward and land it before the right foot. Turn the body 180 degrees to the right, hold the front part of the shaft with the left hand, radial toward the spear butt. (Fig. 6-41) Move the right foot one big step to the right and bend the knee to form the right bow step. At the same time, loosen the left hand grip and pull the spear with the right hand to the lower right to bump forward, force focused on the spearhead. Slip the left hand to the rear of the shaft. Eyes on the spearhead. (Fig. 6-42)

Spear——Behind Back Piercing with Forward Step—— Receive Spear, Parry Inward and Outward, and Thrust with Bow Step

1. Bump the spear to the lower right with the right bow

Fig. 6-36

Fig. 6-37

Fig. 6-38

177

Fig. 6-39

Fig. 6-40

Fig. 6-41

Fig. 6-42

179

**Group Six** Bump Downward with Bow Step———Throat Piercing step. (Fig.6-42)

2. Raise the body, send the spear horizontally to the left with the right hand, loosen the left-hand grip and slip the left hand to near the right hand. (Fig. 6-43) Immediately hold the shaft near the head with the right hand, and pull it horizontally to the right so that the spearhead pierces to the right close to the neck. (Fig. 6-44) Continue to pierce the spear horizontally to the right with the aid of the left hand, and slip the right hand to the spear butt and hold it with one hand. (Fig. 6-45)

3. Extend the right foot outward, turn the body 90 degrees to the right, and hold the spear in the middle with the left hand. (Fig. 6-46)

Move the left foot one step forward, and then the right foot one step forward. At the same time, pull the spear backward with the right hand and turn it inward to change to a backhand grip, radial toward the butt end. Loosen the left-hand grip and slip it forward. (Fig. 6-47, 6-48)

4. Continue from the previous movement. Hold the spear with both hands and raise it overhead to behind the back. (Fig. 6-49) Move the left foot one step forward, and at the same time exert force from the right hand and loosen the left-hand grip so that the spear pierces forward from behind the back and flies out. (Fig. 6-50)

5. Continue from the previous movement, move the right foot one step forward and then the left foot one step forward to grab the flying spear, and bend the knees to form the semi-horse-riding stance. Hold the spear butt with the right hand at the right side of the waist, with the left hand at the middle. (Fig. 6-51)

6. Parry outward, parry inward, and thrust horizontally with the left bow step. (Fig. 6-52, 6-53, 6-54) ( See Fig. 6-3, 6-4, 6-5)

Fig. 6-43

Fig. 6-44

181

Fig. 6-45

Fig. 6-46

Fig. 6-47

Fig. 6-48

183

Fig. 6-49

Fig. 6-50

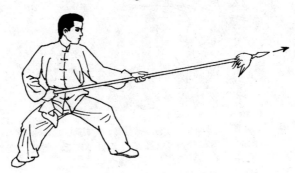

Fig. 6-51

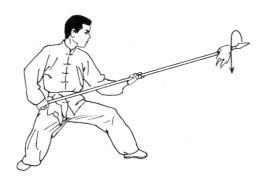

Fig. 6-52

Fig. 6-53

Fig. 6-54

185

**Group Seven** Hold Spear with Semi-Horse-Riding Stance——Lower Outward Parry with Bow Step——Inward Parry with Toe Step——Lower Outward Parry with Backward Bent Legs——Inward Parry with Foot Stamping——Horizontal Flick with Toe Step

1. Hold the spear with both hands while in the semi-horse-riding stance. (Fig. 6-55)

2. Continue from the previous movement. Shift the body weight to the right to form the right bow step. Hold the spear butt with the right hand and turn it over above the head and parry to the lower left with the front of the spear. (Fig. 6-56)

3. Continue from the previous movement. Move the right foot to the left foot to form the right toe step, lower the right hand to waist level and execute the inward parry with the aid of the left hand. (Fig. 6-57)

4. Continue from the previous movement. Raise the right foot backward and bend the knee. While lifting the shaft upward with both hands, execute the lower parry. (Fig. 6-58)

5. Continue from the previous movement. Stamp the right foot by the left foot, and lower both hands to execute the inward parry. (Fig. 6-59)

6. Continue from the previous movement. Move the left foot forward to form the toe step. Hold the spear butt with the right hand at the right side of the neck, slip the left hand forward and hold it tightly to execute the horizontal flick to the back lower left. (Fig. 6-60)

**Group Eight** Hold Spear with Semi Horse-Riding Stance——Horizontal Thrust with Turning Trunk and Circular Walking Step——Jab with Butt and Feet Together——Parry and Thrust with Bow Step——Flick with Empty Step

1. Hold the spear with both hands while in the semi-horse-riding stance. (Fig. 6-61)

2. Continue from the previous movement. Straighten both

186

Fig. 6-55

Fig. 6-56

187

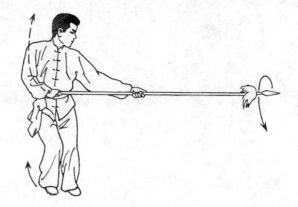

Fig. 6-57

Fig. 6-58

188

Fig. 6-59

Fig. 6-60

189

legs, pull the spear butt to the right with the right hand, and slip the left hand to the front of the shaft. (Fig. 6-62)

3. Continue from the previous movement. Use the combined force of both hands to thrust the spear butt horizontally from right to left and slip the right hand to the front of the shaft, at the same time the body turns 90 degrees to the left. (Fig. 6-63)

4. Continue from the previous movement. Move the right foot forward to the left circularly, exchange hand grips, and pull the spear with the right hand backward to the right. (Fig. 6-64)

5. Continue from the previous movement. Move the lcft foot forward to the left circularly, use the combined force of the hands to thrust the spearhead horizontally from right to left. (Fig. 6-65)

6. Continue from the previous movement. Move the right foot forward to the left circularly, exchange hand grips, hold the spear butt end with the right hand, and the middle of the shaft with the left hand. (Fig. 6-66)

7. Continue from the previous movement. Move the left foot to the right foot and put the feet together. Change the left hand to the backhand grip, hold the shaft at the middle, and bend it in front of the chest. Slip the right hand to jab the spear butt horizontally to the right. (Fig. 6-67)

8. Continue from the previous movement. Slip the right hand to the butt end, hold the spear with both hands in the semi-horse-riding stance to parry outward and inward, (Fig. 6-68, 6-69) and thrust with the bow step. (Fig. 6-70)

9. Continue from the previous movement. Move the left foot one half step backward to form the left empty step, and use the combined force of both hands to flick upward with the spearhead. (Fig. 6-71)

Fig. 6-61

Fig. 6-62

Fig. 6-63

Fig. 6-64

Fig. 6-65

Fig. 6-66

Fig. 6-67

Fig. 6-68

194

Fig. 6-69

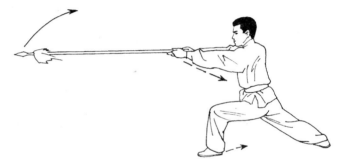

Fig. 6-70

Fig. 6-71

**Group Nine** Thrust Downward with Single Hand——Pull Spear with Back Cross Step——Hold Spear with Semi-Horse-Riding Stance——Coil Spear with Forward Step——Thrust with Jump and Half Body Turn

Initial posture: Hold the spear with feet together. (Fig. 6-72)

1. Thrust the spear to the lower left with one hand. (Fig. 6-73)

2. Move the left foot one big step obliquely backward behind the body to the left and bend the left leg to a half squat, toes outward, to form the back cross step. At the same time, hold the spear butt with the right hand and pull it to outside the right shoulder, spearhead on the ground and the shaft lying obliquely across in front of the body. Extend the left hand horizontally to the left with a flat palm. Eyes looking ahead to the left. (Fig. 6-74)

3. Land the right foot obliquely forward to the right and bend the legs to a half squat to form the semi-horse-riding stance. At the same time, hold the middle of the shaft with the left hand, and the butt end with the right hand. Lower the spear butt and withdraw it to the waist. (Fig. 6-75)

4. Raise the body slightly, and move the right foot one step forward. Hold the spear with both hands to circle the spearhead one rotation counterclockwise. (Fig. 6-76)

5. Move the left foot forward, and then the right foot forward. Continue to coil the spear, one rotation each step for five or seven steps begin-

Fig. 6-72

Fig. 6-73

Fig. 6-74

Fig. 6-75

197

ning with the right foot. (Fig. 6-77, 6-78)

6. Hold the spear with both hands, move the left foot one step forward and stamp the foot on the ground, then jump up and turn the body 180 degrees in the air. At the same time, thrust the spear horizontally forward with one hand, change the left hand into a palm and move it backward to the left. (Fig. 6-79, 6-80)

**Group Ten** Hold Spear with Semi-Horse-Riding Stance——Jab Spear Butt with Back Cross Step——Cut with Forward Step——Left and Right Figures——Left Outward Parry and Right Cut——Return Thrust with Seated Stance

Initial posture: Hold the spear with feet together. (Fig. 6-1)

1. Hold the spear while in the semi-horse-riding stance. (Fig. 6-81)

2. Move the left foot backward to the right behind the right leg. At the same time, slip the left hand and the right hand, one after another, to the middle of the shaft to jab horizontally to the right with the spear butt, force focused on the butt end and eyes on the spear butt. (Fig. 6-82)

3. Turn the body to the front and move the left foot one step forward. At the same time, slip the right hand to the butt end to pull the spear to the lower left in front of the body. (Fig. 6-83) Immediately move the right foot one big step forward, hold the spear with both hands to cut upward and forward from the lower and backward left, force focused on the front of the shaft. Withdraw the right hand to the right side of the waist and bend the left arm slightly, palm facing downward, to hold the shaft. (Fig. 6-84)

4. Withdraw the right foot one half step. At the same time, slip both hands to the middle of the shaft to circle the spearhead downward in front of the body to behind the body on the right side, the spear butt moving upward from behind the body to upper forward in front of the head, hold the spear with

Fig. 6-76

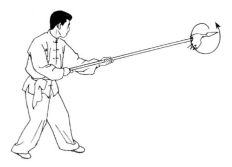

Fig. 6-77

Fig. 6-78

199

Fig. 6-79

Fig. 6-80

200

Fig. 6-81

Fig. 6-82

201

Fig. 6-83

Fig. 6-84

hands crossed. (Fig. 6-85)

5. Turn the trunk to the left and hold the spear with both hands to circle figures vertically in front of the body. Circle the spear one or more times on each side of the body. (Fig. 6-86, 6-87, 6-88)

6. When the left foot is in front, stop circling and slip the right hand to the spear butt and hold the middle of the shaft with the left hand. (Fig. 6-89) Immediately turn the body 90 degrees to the right, bend the right leg to a half squat and bend the left leg slightly, heel raised. At the same time, hold the spear with both hands and turn the wrists above the head while lifting the spear to parry outward on the left side of the body. (Fig. 6-90)

7. Turn the trunk to the right and at the same time hold the spear with both hands and move it upward from the left to cut down on the right side, force focused on the front of the shaft. (Fig. 6-91)

8. Turn the trunk to the left, stand with feet apart and hold the spear with both hands to circle the spearhead from the right upward and to the left, shaft lying horizontally above and in front of the head. (Fig. 6-92)

9. Turn the trunk to the left and cross the legs to squat down to the cross-legged sitting stance. At the same time, hold the spear with the right hand to thrust it to the lower front, arm turned inward and palm facing downward. Change the left hand into a palm and extend it backward to the left side of the body. Eyes on the spearhead. (Fig. 6-93)

Fig. 6-85

Fig. 6-86

Fig. 6-87

Fig. 6-88

205

Fig. 6-89

Fig. 6-90

206

Fig. 6-91

Fig. 6-92

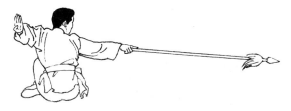

Fig. 6-93

207

**图书在版编目(CIP)数据**

枪术入门:英文/邱丕相著. —北京:外文出版社,1999
(中国武术丛书)
ISBN 7 - 119 - 01392 - 0

Ⅰ.枪… Ⅱ.邱… Ⅲ.枪术(武术) - 基本知识 - 中国 - 英文 Ⅳ.G852.23

中国版本图书馆 CIP 数据核字 (98) 第 05626 号

责任编辑 贾先锋
封面设计 朱振安
插图绘制 李士仮

外文出版社网页:
http://www.flp.com.cn
外文出版社电子邮件地址:
info@flp.com.cn
sales@flp.com.cn

**枪术入门**

邱丕相  著

*

ⓒ外文出版社
外文出版社出版
(中国北京百万庄大街 24 号)
邮政编码 100037
北京外文印刷厂印刷
中国国际图书贸易总公司发行
(中国北京车公庄西路 35 号)
北京邮政信箱第 399 号  邮政编码 100044
1999 年(大 32 开)第 1 版
1999 年第 1 版第 1 次印刷
(英)
ISBN 7 - 119 - 01392 - 0/G·14(外)
03500(平)
7 - E - 3098P